For my daughters
Kavya & Avni
who are my poetry
& my world.

New Moon
Rising

A collection of poems by Anuradha Gupta

One cold January morning, I woke up to Life.

It was as if that morning Life had caught the sun at just the perfect angle and was shining with a radiance I had not seen before.

For weeks after that it was like being in love. I noticed its every little nuance, heard every chirp, rejoiced at every new blossom, marveled at every stray cloud and even at every airplane that flew noisily overhead.

I couldn't understand it.

The year had begun on an ominous note and bad news was continuing to stream in from all sides. I was surrounded by pain, loss, grief.

Yet there I was, in the midst of all the sadness, completely enchanted by the world around me. It was beautiful. So real, so heartbreakingly transient.

I sought desperately to hold on to some of that beauty while I could, watching every moment as it passed.

Hidden in one of those moments was the beginnings of this book. A desire to create something to remember life by.

I took a collection of verses, musings from a quiet place and set about creating this mosaic of poems and paintings. While the words had flowed spontaneously, the art I had to learn and took a lot longer. They are, however, both true unselfconscious expressions of my inner self.

As I immersed myself in this project, memories flooded back. People and places I had known and loved, a childhood tucked away in a little pocket of heaven in small town India, summers spent at my grandmother's with a horde of cousins, the monsoons that followed. Friends I had grown up with and the friends I grew up to make, the birth of my daughters, the travels.

My whole life, as it were, gathered around me. The dark moments were there too, rendering the shadows against which all that was good glowed. I shall forever be warmed by that glow.

In sharing my book with you, I wish you too a life lived and celebrated in little moments.

Seasons

Stretching all around me

Summer draped over dusty earth

A sky full of blue sky

We don't say a word
The mountains, the valley and I
As the day slips quietly by

On my verandah

a summer's evening

breathless from the day

glowing

fading into the night

her eyes are bright, smiling

and around me a thousand stories

like fireflies are gathering

All night long it rains
Pouring its heart out
Rain

Relentless unceasing
Dark with longing
Rain

Pounding the earth
Crushing insisting
Rain

Till earth undone melts
Drowning her softly
Rain

When the rain came back
I was waiting

I knew there would be
One last meeting.

Framed
    In my Starbucks window
An early autumn scene.

Runaway leaves
    Chase each other
Down the street and
    Huddle up on a pavement
Like a bunch of giggling kids.

Looking out from within
    I watch the seasons turning
Hot chocolate warming.

The mornings come later now
Long after the alarm's gone
I catch the sun sneaking in
Sideways, over the garden fence
Where have you been? I ask
He doesn't say
Just smiles at me
Then winks

They stand tall dark defiant

Stripped bare to the bark

Lining the wintery park

Throwing up their arms

To the cold stern sky

As if to say, look at us now

This is who we are

This is who we are

It gets harder each year

To let the year go

I walk it to the door

And we stand chatting

About this that and everything

Memories mostly, happenings

Dodging the goodbyes

and waiting ...

Spaces

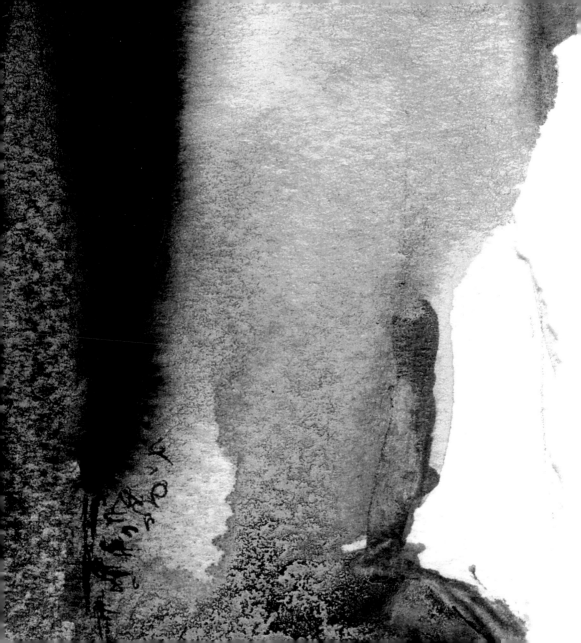

I walk back from the desert
 Filled with its emptiness

Behind me desert winds sigh.

All that was is now nothing
Just grains of sand rising
In silent waves and falling

Yearning moon

Long through the desert night
Restless sands shift

Shadows

शॅडोज

I found a full moon
Looking into my kitchen
Wide-eyed and sullen.
Come in, I said
I know what it's like
To be awake all night.

Did you see the moon
Fallen in the lake?
I scooped it out
Frozen, dripping wet.
Then on the black night sky
Hung it out to dry.

There
where the sky melts into the sea
    and fishes swim with stars on their backs
I've seen the moon come down for a walk.

At times, I chase after it
The pale moon
At times, it follows me
Winding through my streets.

How long must we play
This game of hide and seek?

unSpoken

अन स्पोकन

In this moment of loving
I am all that and I am all this
I am me, I am you, I am us
In this moment of being
I am all this and nothing

In your arms
I lose myself
In your arms
I find myself

My breath strung
Upon your breath
What is life now
I wonder
And what is death?

I leave you this much
a handful of sky,
a few stars, one half moon,
a lazy afternoon,
on the floor
a night carelessly strewn,
a rain song drying in the sun,
tales of distant lands
and of course words
so many words.

Bombay.   24. Dec 1904.

The place to spend a 'appy day

self

सेल्फ

I dream that dream again
I'm folding up on myself
Precise practiced folds
Corners tucked in and
Pressed down
Making triangles
Then squares
And triangles again
Until I am
A butterfly
With paper wings
And a mad desire to fly

at the very edge of things
where the lines begin to blur
and curved becomes straight
where blue skies spill into space
and space becomes nothingness
where time warps and
now becomes *then*
becomes *now* again
is where you will find
it all begins to make sense

I shall wrap myself in ochre now
and let the rest drop.
The silks, the gold
the bangles and bells.
Everything that I hold
and all that holds me.

You say I am crazy.
But what do you know
of walking barefoot and free.

Can you hear in my heart
The beating drums, O Krishna
On my breath your flute?

With bells on my toes I dance.

Like the blue sky
Slipping into the sea
He enters me
And I become
The swirling sky
And endless sea.

In the dark of my heart
I found my Self
A new moon rising.

Notes

Some of the poems are very Indian in their sensibilities and carry references which, if you are less acquainted with the sub-continent, may be lost on you. Hence a few notes.

Dedication Kavya & Avni, the names of my daughters, mean 'poetry' and 'the earth' respectively in Sanskrit.

Page 12   The rain from my memory is the torrential rain of the monsoons.

Page 13   A month or so after the monsoons have departed and the October heat is rising we sometimes get a sudden sharp shower out of the blue. I love that unexpected rain.

Page 35   The moon in most Indian languages is masculine and often symbolises the lover or the object of one's desire.

Page 51   In Buddhism and Hinduism, ochre or saffron represents renunciation. Hence monks and yogis wear ochre robes.

Page 52   The peacock feather is one of Krishna's favourite things.

Page 53   Krishna the dark hued god is often coloured blue in paintings.
           Blue also represents spirituality in Hinduism.

Page 54   In India the new moon night is in reality a no-moon night. You can't see the
           moon but hidden somewhere in the darkness is the imperceptible sliver of
           light. The beginning of a new phase.

Title page   The crescent moon bindi, is painted by the women of Maharashtra on their
           foreheads. A symbol that reminds me of my roots.

Some months ago this book was just a dream.

To make it a reality I leaned on the generosity of my family, my friends and their friends for everything from advice to technical support. My thanks to all of you who helped.

I am deeply grateful to:

John Dougill, for hearing my voice and believing in it long before I did. But for you, the poems might never have happened.

Val Wolstenholme Clay for giving me the courage to express myself with art and raising my artistic quotient to an all time high.

Toni Marshall for helping me design this book page by page, edit after edit with enormous patience and good humour.

Sangeeta for getting as excited about the book as I was and for providing the much needed scaffolding.

Roz, Jackie, Laura and all the writers at Swanwick Writer's Summer School for inspiring me year after year.

Rajesh for making another, one of my earliest dreams come true.

My parents Vasant and Kavita for always being there and all my wonderful family and friends for just being. You enrich my life in more ways than I can say.

Anuradha Gupta was born in India in 1971 and grew up there. She moved away some years ago and has since lived in Connecticut, Prague and now London which she calls home. When she is not pre-occupied with being a mum she freelances as a travel writer and writes a blog on Hinduism. You can visit the blog at www.allabouthinduism.com

First published in 2013 by Anuradha Gupta

Text and illustrations copyright ©Anuradha Gupta.

The moral right of the author/illustrator has been asserted

All rights reserved.

A catalogue record of this book is available from the British Library

ISBN 978-0-9576954-0-5

Book design by Toni Marshall & Anuradha Gupta

Printed and bound in India by Pragati Offset, Hyderabad.